A
POEM
For
EVERYONE

OXFORD
UNIVERSITY PRESS

Great Clarendon Street, Oxford OX2 6DP

Oxford University Press is a department of the University of Oxford.
It furthers the University's objective of excellence in research, scholarship,
and education by publishing worldwide in

Oxford New York

Auckland Cape Town Dar es Salaam Hong Kong Karachi
Kuala Lumpur Madrid Melbourne Mexico City Nairobi
New Delhi Shanghai Taipei Toronto

With offices in

Argentina Austria Brazil Chile Czech Republic France Greece
Guatemala Hungary Italy Japan Poland Portugal Singapore
South Korea Switzerland Thailand Turkey Ukraine Vietnam

Oxford is a registered trade mark of Oxford University Press
in the UK and in certain other countries

British Library Cataloguing in Publication Data available

ISBN-13: 978-0-19-276251-1
ISBN-10: 0-19-276251-6

3 5 7 9 10 8 6 4 2

Typeset by Mary Tudge (Typesetting Services)
Designed by Louise Millar

Printed and bound in Great Britain by
Mackays of Chatham plc, Chatham, Kent

A
POEM
For
EVERYONE

Michael Harrison and
Christopher Stuart-Clark

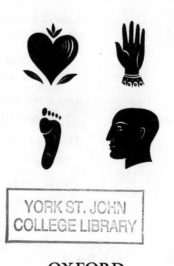

OXFORD
UNIVERSITY PRESS

Contents

Mum'll Be Coming Home Today

MICHAEL ROSEN

Mum'll be coming home today.
It's three weeks she's been away.
When Dad's alone
all we eat
is cold meat
which I don't like
and he burns the toast I want just-brown
and I hate taking the ash-can down.

He's mended the door
from the little fight
on Thursday night
so it doesn't show
and can we have grilled tomatoes
Spanish onions and roast potatoes
and will you sing me 'I'll never more roam'
when I'm in bed, when you've come home?

Mum's reply

If you like your toast
done just-brown
then take it out
before it burns.
You hate taking the ash-can down?
Well now you know
what I know
so we might as well take turns.

But now I'm back,
yes let's have grilled tomatoes
Spanish onions and roast potatoes
because you know
when I was away
I wanted nothing more
than be back here
and see you all.

Nobody Knows But Mother

MARY MORRISON

How many buttons are missing today?
   Nobody knows but Mother.
How many playthings are strewn in her way?
   Nobody knows but Mother.
How many thimbles and spools has she missed?
How many burns on each fat little fist?
How many bumps to be cuddled and kissed?
   Nobody knows but Mother.

How many hats has she hunted today?
   Nobody knows but Mother.
Carelessly hiding themselves in the hay—
   Nobody knows but Mother.
How many handkerchiefs wilfully strayed?
How many ribbons for each little maid?
How for her care can a mother be paid?
   Nobody knows but Mother.

How many muddy shoes all in a row?
   Nobody knows but Mother.
How many stockings to darn, do you know?
   Nobody knows but Mother.
How many little torn aprons to mend?
How many hours of toil must she spend?
What is the time when her day's work shall end?
   Nobody knows but Mother.

How many lunches for Tommy and Sam?
   Nobody knows but Mother.
Cookies and apples and blackberry jam—
   Nobody knows but Mother.

Nourishing dainties for every 'sweet tooth',
Toddling Dottie or dignified Ruth—
How much love sweetens the labor, forsooth?
   Nobody knows but Mother.

How many cares does a mother's heart know?
   Nobody knows but Mother.
How many joys from her mother love flow?
   Nobody knows but Mother.
How many prayers for each little white bed?
How many tears for her babes has she shed?
How many kisses for each curly head?
   Nobody knows but Mother.

Squeezes
BRIAN PATTEN

We love to squeeze bananas,
We love to squeeze ripe plums,
And when they are feeling sad
We love to squeeze our mums.

Happy Birthday from Bennigans
JULIE O'CALLAGHAN

Why did you do it, Mother?
I told you—didn't I—that I'd go with you
to a restaurant for my birthday
on one condition: Don't go and blab
to the waitress it's my BIG DAY.
But you had to go and tell her.
God, what if somebody had seen me?
I realize that you and Daddy
simply do not care if you ruin my reputation.
I almost thought for a teensy second
you had restrained yourself for once.
But no. You and your big mouth.
'Hip, hop, happy, b, birth, day,
hap, hap, happy, Happy Birthday to You!':
a zero girl, singing a zero song
at the top of her nothingness of a voice.
'All of us at Bennigans hope it's a special day!'
All of them, Mother, not just some.
That's IT for birthdays from now on.
Next year I'll be celebrating by myself.

Mother Love
STEVIE SMITH

Mother love is a mighty benefaction
The prop of the world and its population
If mother love died the world would rue it
No money would bring the women to it.

Father Says
MICHAEL ROSEN

Father says
Never
let
me
see
you
doing
that
again
father says
tell you once
tell you a thousand times
come hell or high water
his finger drills my shoulder
never let me see you doing that again

My brother knows all his phrases off by heart
so we practise them in bed at night.

Mum Dad and Me

JAMES BERRY

My parents grew among palmtrees,
in sunshine strong and clear.
I grow in weather that's pale,
misty, watery or plain cold,
around back streets of London.

Dad swam in warm sea, at my age.
I swim in a roofed pool.
Mum—she still doesn't swim.

Mum went to an open village market
at my age. I go to a covered
arcade one with her now.
Dad works most Saturdays.

At my age Dad played
cricket with friends.
Mum helped her mum, or talked
shouting halfway up a hill.
Now I read or talk on the phone.

With her friends Mum's mum washed
clothes on a river-stone. Now
washing-machine washes our clothes.
We save time to eat to TV,
never speaking.

My dad longed for a freedom in Jamaica.
I want a greater freedom.
Mum prays for us, always.

Mum goes to church
some evenings and Sundays.
I go to the library.
Dad goes for his darts at the local.

Mum walked everywhere, at my age.
Dad rode a donkey.
Now I take a bus
or catch the underground train.

My Dad, Your Dad

KIT WRIGHT

My dad's fatter than your dad,
Yes, my dad's fatter than yours:
If he eats any more he won't fit in the house,
He'll have to live out of doors.

Yes, but my dad's balder than your dad,
My dad's balder, OK,
He's only got two hairs left on his head
And both are turning grey.

Ah, but my dad's thicker than your dad,
My dad's thicker, all right.
He has to look at his watch to see
If it's noon or the middle of the night.

Yes, but my dad's more boring than your dad.
If he ever starts counting sheep
When he can't get to sleep at night, he finds
It's the sheep that go to sleep.

But my dad doesn't mind your dad.
Mine quite likes yours too.
I suppose they don't always think much of US!
That's true, I suppose, that's true.

Sunday Fathers

JOHN CORBEN

I used to notice them,
one of the Sunday sights:
fathers visiting their children
and walking them in parks
or sitting over milk-shakes
making careful conversation.

I saw a pair one Sunday
looking in a shop window,
I thought, but the boy's eyes
were curtained with tears
and the father's arms were shut
out by more than the week.

Now I try not to see them:
such a shadow on the sun's day

My Little Sister

ANN BONNER

My sister
and I
always
fight.

I'm sure she's
wrong. I
think I'm
right.

She pinches my
toys
when I'm not
there

she cheats at
games.
She's never
fair.

She leaves her
clothes
all over the
place

if I complain
she pulls a
face.

Every
morning
I have to
wait

to take her
to school . . .
we're always
late . . .

but however
naughty
she can
be

nothing
must hurt her.
She's smaller
than me.

Twin Sisters
IRENE RAWNSLEY

My sisters
are pictures in a pop-up book,
only made of cardboard
if you care to look.

Visitors
admire their lacy dresses,
matching noses,
curly tresses;

but if nobody's looking
the smiles fold down
into twin, mean faces,
sulky frowns.

They're pop-up pictures,
I'm sure of that.
I'd like to shut the pages
and squash them flat.

New Baby

JACKIE KAY

My baby brother makes so much noise
that the Rottweiler next door
phoned up to complain.

My baby brother makes so much noise
that all the big green frogs
came out the drains.

My baby brother makes so much noise
that the rats and the mice
wore headphones.

My baby brother makes so much noise
that I can't ask my mum a question,
so much noise that sometimes

I think of sitting the cat on top of him
in his pretty little cot with all his teddies.
But even the cat is terrified of his cries.

So I have devised a plan. A soundproof room.
A telephone to talk to my mum.
A small lift to receive food and toys.

Thing is, it will cost a fortune.
The other thing is, the frogs have gone.
It's not bad now. Not that I like him or anything.

Brother

MARY ANN HOBERMAN

I had a little brother
And I brought him to my mother
And I said I want another
Little brother for a change.
But she said don't be a bother
so I took him to my father
And I said this little bother
Of a brother's very strange.

But he said one little brother
Is exactly like another
And every little brother
Misbehaves a bit he said.
So I took the little brother
From my mother and my father
And I put the little bother
Of a brother back to bed.

The Whistler

JUNE CREBBIN

My little brother is almost six,
He's good at maths and magic tricks,
He's quite a neat writer,
He can hop and jump and pull funny faces,
He can do top buttons and tie his laces,
He's a fearless fighter.

But he wanted to whistle—and though he tried
Till his face went red and he almost cried,
He still couldn't do it,
So he asked me how and I said: 'Make an O
With your mouth and then, very gently, blow
A whistle through it.'

And he did—but now the trouble is
My little brother practises
All day long,
He sucks in his cheeks, he puffs and blows,
Whatever he's doing, his whistling goes
On and on . . . and on . . .

The Magic Handbag

MICHAEL RICHARDS

When Granny comes to stay
She brings her black handbag.
As soon as she's in through the door,
'Let me see what I've got here,'
She says.
She opens her bag
And in goes her hand
And out come my favourite sweets.

If I need a pencil to draw the cat,
If she needs scissors to cut my nails,
If I scrape my knee and need a plaster,
'Let me see what I've got here,'
She says.
She opens her bag
And in goes her hand
And out comes whatever I need.

At home her bag behaves itself
And nothing strange is ever let out.
But once Granny and I are off on a walk
Just anything can come out of that bag.

One hot afternoon we are in the park.
'I'm tired and I'm hot,' I say.
'Let me see what I've got here,'
She says.
She opens her bag
And in goes her hand
And out comes a cone of strawberry ice-cream.

Suddenly we hear a noise, a humming brown noise.
'Bees,' says Granny, 'a swarm of bees.'
'Let me see what I've got here,'
She says.

She opens her bag
But she doesn't put in her hand.
She holds it open and, with a noise
Like the bath emptying,
All the bees swarm in.
'There,' says Granny, and shuts her bag,
'Let's go home for a cup of tea.'

It was a long way home. 'What we need,'
I say, 'is a short cut.'
'Let me see what I've got here,'
She says.
She opens her bag
And puts it down on the pavement.
She takes hold of my hand, and then,
And then we are in a huge dark cave.
There's a slight buzzing sound
And a smell of honey. 'Come on!'
Says Granny. 'We'll be late for tea.'

We step out into the sunlight
And there we are outside home,
And in we go, in time for tea.
'Let me see what I've got here,'
She says.
She opens her bag
And in goes her hand
And out comes a jar of honey.

The Older the Violin
the Sweeter the Tune

JOHN AGARD

Me Granny old
Me Granny wise
stories shine like a moon
from inside she eyes.

Me Granny can dance
Me Granny can sing
but she can't play violin.

Yet she always saying,
'Dih older dih violin
de sweeter de tune.'

Me Granny must be wiser
than the man inside the moon.

My Grannies

JUNE CREBBIN

I hate it, in the holiday,
When Grandma brings her pets to stay—
Her goat, her pig, her seven rats
Scare our dog and chase our cats.
Her budgies bite, her parrots shout—
And guess who has to clean them out?

My other Gran, the one I like,
Always brings her motor-bike,
And when she takes me for a ride
To picnic in the countryside,
We zoom up hills and whizz round bends—
I hate it when her visit ends!

Grannie

VERNON SCANNELL

I stayed with her when I was six then went
To live elsewhere when I was eight years old.
For ages I remembered her faint scent
Of lavender, the way she'd never scold
No matter what I'd done, and most of all
The way her smile seemed, somehow, to enfold
My whole world like a warm, protective shawl.

I knew that I was safe when she was near,
She was so tall, so wide, so large, she would
Stand mountainous between me and my fear,
Yet oh, so gentle, and she understood
Every hope and dream I ever had.
She praised me lavishly when I was good,
But never punished me when I was bad.

Years later war broke out and I became
A soldier and was wounded while in France.
Back home in hospital, still very lame,
I realized suddenly that circumstance
Had brought me close to that small town where she
Was living still. And so I seized the chance
To write and ask if she could visit me.

She came. And I still vividly recall
The shock that I received when she appeared
That dark cold day. Huge grannie was so small!
A tiny, frail, old lady. It was weird.
She hobbled through the ward to where I lay
And drew quite close and, hesitating, peered.
And then she smiled: and love lit up the day.

Seeing Granny
JAMES BERRY

Toothless, she kisses
with fleshly lips
rounded, like mouth
of a bottle, all wet.

She bruises your face
almost, with two
loving tree-root hands.

She makes you sit, fixed.
She then stuffs you
with boiled pudding and lemonade.

She watches you feed
on her food. She milks
you dry of answers
about the goat she gave you.

'You're Right,' Said Grandad

JOAN POULSON

I went round to help him
the day he moved
it was an upstairs flat
this old one he had
he'd lived there
with Gran
for twenty-nine years
they told him
it was time
he had a move

we laughed, me and Grandad
at the dark front room
'Like an old fox's den,'
I said. 'Just wait until
you're sitting in that bright
light room—with all
that glass. You'll be able to
sit and watch
everybody pass.'
'You're right, I will,'
said Grandad.

we laughed, me and Grandad
at the garden round the back.
'Like a jungle, at its best,'
I said. 'Just wait until
you're resting in your
new place. No more
hacking-out
a deckchair space.

No weeds annoying you.
There'll be plenty
company for you, too.
They'll sit outside
the people from
the other bungalows.
sit on the benches
chat with you.'
'You're right, they will,'
said Grandad.

We laughed, me and Grandad
at his rickety old shed.
'Like something from
a horror film!' I said.
'You'll be much better off
without it. And didn't
the doctor tell you
all that sawdust
wasn't good, got on your chest?
And we've all got wooden stools
and things, enough to last
a lifetime, anyway.
Our Sheryll really loved
that box you made her.
All those different
colours, different woods.
Dad says you've been a
first-rate craftsman
in your time.'
'He's right, I have,'
said Grandad.
'Yes, I have.'

Grandpa Never Sleeps

MARK BURGESS

Grandpa doesn't sleep at night,
He never sleeps a wink.
Instead he tinkers with the car
Or mends the kitchen sink.

Sometimes he picks the rhubarb
Or polishes the floor.
And other nights he's shopping
At the local all-night store.

Last night he papered half the hall
And built a garden shed.
But when the rest of us got up
He *didn't* go to bed.

I don't know how he does it,
He's always on the go.
Grandpa never sleeps AT ALL—
At least, I think that's so . . .

Aunt Sue's Stories

LANGSTON HUGHES

Aunt Sue has a head full of stories.
Aunt Sue has a whole heart full of stories.
Summer nights on the front porch
Aunt Sue cuddles a brown-faced child to her bosom
And tells him stories.

Black slaves
Working in the hot sun,
And black slaves
Walking in the dewy night,
And black slaves
Singing sorrow songs on the banks of a mighty river
Mingle themselves softly
In the flow of old Aunt Sue's voice,
Mingle themselves softly
In the dark shadows that cross and recross
Aunt Sue's stories.

And the dark-faced child, listening,
Knows that Aunt Sue's stories are real stories.
He knows that Aunt Sue never got her stories
Out of any book at all,
But that they came
Right out of her own life.

The dark-faced child is quiet
Of a summer night
Listening to Aunt Sue's stories.

Uncle Alfred's Long Jump

GARETH OWEN

When Mary Rand
Won the Olympic Long Jump,
My Auntie Hilda
Paced out the distance
On the pavement outside her house.
'Look at that!'
She shouted challengingly
At the dustman, the milkman, the grocer,
Two Jehovah's Witnesses
And a male St Bernard
Who happened to be passing,
'A girl, a girl did that;
If you men are so clever
Let's see what you can do.'
Nobody took up the challenge
Until Uncle Alfred trudged home
Tired from the office
Asking for his tea.
'Our Mary did that!'
Said Auntie Hilda proudly
Pointing from the lamppost
To the rose-bush by her gate.
'You men are so clever,
Let's see how near
That rose-bush you end up.'
His honour and manhood at stake,
Uncle Alfred put down his bowler
His brief-case and his brolly
And launched himself
Into a fifty yard run-up.
'End up at that rose-bush,'

He puffed mockingly,
'I'll show you where I'll end up.'
His take off from the lamppost
Was a thing of beauty,
But where he ended up
Was in The Royal Infirmary
With both legs in plaster.
'Some kind of record!'
He said proudly to the bone specialist;
While through long nights
In a ward full of coughs and snoring
He dreamed about the washing line
And of how to improve
His high jump technique.

Uncle and Auntie

JOHN HEGLEY

my auntie gives me a colouring book and crayons
I begin to colour
after a while auntie leans over and says
you've gone over the lines
what do you think they're there for
eh?
some kind of statement is it?
going to be a rebel are we?
your auntie gives you a lovely present
and you have to go and ruin it
I begin to cry
my uncle gives me a hanky and some blank paper
do some doggies of your own he says
I begin to colour
when I have done
he looks over
and says they are all very good
he is lying
only some of them are

Purple William

A. E. HOUSMAN

The hideous hue which William is
Was not originally his:
So long as William told the truth
He was a usual-coloured youth.

He now is purple. One fine day
His tender father chanced to say
'What colour is a whelp, and why?'
'Purple,' was William's false reply.

'Pooh,' said his Pa, 'You silly elf,
It's no more purple than yourself
Dismiss the notion from your head.'
'I, too, am purple,' William said.

And he *was* purple. With a yell
His mother off the sofa fell
Exclaiming, 'William's purple! Oh!'
William replied, 'I told you so.'

His parents, who could not support
The pungency of this retort,
Died with a simultaneous groan.
The purple orphan was alone.

Lies

CAROL ANN DUFFY

I like to go out for the day and tell lies.
The day should be overcast
with a kind of purple, electric edge to the clouds;
and not too hot or cold,
but cool.
I turn up the collar of my coat
and narrow my eyes.

I meet someone—
a girl from school perhaps—
I like them shy.
Then I start to lie
as we walk along Tennyson Drive kicking a can.
She listens hard,
her split strawberry mouth moist and mute;
my weasel words
sparking the little lights in her spectacles.
At the corner of Coleridge Place
I watch her run,
thrilled, fast, chasing her breath,
home to her mum.

Bus-stops I like,
with long, bored, footsore, moaning queues.
I lie to them
in my shrill, confident voice,
till the number 8 or 11 takes them away
and I stand and stare at the bend in Longfellow Road,
alone in the day.

At the end of the darkening afternoon
I head for home,
watching the lights turn on in truthful rooms
where mothers come and go
with plates of cakes,
and TV sets shuffle their bright cartoons.
Then I knock on the door of 21 Wordsworth Way,
and while I wait
I watch a spaceship zoom away overhead
and see the faint half-smile of the distant moon.
They let me in.
And who, they want to know, do I think I am?
Exactly where have I been? With whom? And why?
The thing with me—
I like to come home after a long day out
and lie.

Night Boy

MATTHEW SWEENEY

After the cat went out
and the moon sat on the hill
and the sea drowned a lorry
that broke down
                    stealing sand,
little, skinny George awoke.

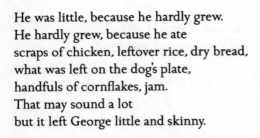

He was little, because he hardly grew.
He hardly grew, because he ate
scraps of chicken, leftover rice, dry bread,
what was left on the dog's plate,
handfuls of cornflakes, jam.
That may sound a lot
but it left George little and skinny.

What about mealtimes? I hear you ask.
Mealtimes, for George, were sleeptimes
most of the year. That's right,
he slept all day,
                    got up at night.

What about school? you're saying.
I know, I know what you're like.
What do you know about stars?
Does the sea glow at night
like a green watch-dial?
Ask George, he'll tell you.
He'll even write it down
and read it to you, by torchlight,
and then he'll count the stars.

Blame the holidays, his Gran said,
they're too long.
George lived with his Gran,
George, the sleeper-in
who'd slept in so long, so often,
that now he woke at night
when Gran was asleep.

What did he do at night?
He went to the beach,
lit driftwood fires,
stood in a cave and waited
for spies in submarines
to land.
      He climbed hills
and aeroplane-spotted,
especially small ones
landing in fields.

He hid in ditches
and eavesdropped on strangers.
He woke the neighbour's donkey
and galloped round the field.

He lay on a haystack
and watched the dawn.
Then he yawned
                and went to bed.

And if he met Gran on the stairs,
Good day, was what he said.

Brendon Gallacher
(for my brother, Maxie)

JACKIE KAY

He was seven and I was six, my Brendon Gallacher.
He was Irish and I was Scottish, my Brendon Gallacher.
His father was in prison; he was a cat burglar.
My father was a communist party full-time worker.
He has six brothers and I had one, my Brendon Gallacher.

He would hold my hand and take me by the river
Where we'd talk all about his family being poor.
He'd get his mum out of Glasgow when he got older.
A wee holiday some place nice. Some place far.
I'd tell my mum about my Brendon Gallacher.

How his mum drank and his daddy was a cat burglar.
And she'd say, 'Why not have him round to dinner?'
No, no, I'd say, he's got big holes in his trousers.
I like meeting him by the burn in the open air.
Then one day after we'd been friends two years,

One day when it was pouring and I was indoors,
My mum says to me, 'I was talking to Mrs Moir
Who lives next door to your Brendon Gallacher
Didn't you say his address was 24 Novar?
She says there are no Gallachers at 24 Novar

There never have been any Gallachers next door.'
And he died then, my Brendon Gallacher,
Flat out on my bedroom floor, his spiky hair,
His impish grin, his funny flapping ear.
Oh Brendon, oh my Brendon Gallacher.

I Asked the Little Boy Who Cannot See

ANON.

I asked the little boy who cannot see,
'And what is colour like?'
'Why, green,' said he,
'Is like the rustle when the wind blows through
The forest; running water, that is blue;
And red is like a trumpet sound; and pink
Is like the smell of roses; and I think
That purple must be like a thunderstorm;
And yellow is like something soft and warm;
And white is a pleasant stillness when you lie
And dream.'

My Friend Thelma

RUSSELL HOBAN

Such a friend as my friend Thelma everyone has not.
Such a friend as my friend Thelma is who I have got.

She's the one who always knows
In the winter when it snows
That the school bus will get through,
Calls up kids like me and you
So that we won't think the bus
Isn't coming. Hopeful us.

Thelma, when the ice is new,
Always says, 'I think that you
Ought to try it,' and I do,
And it's thin, and I go through.
When I get home sopping wet,
Into trouble's what I get.

Thelma will drop in on me
When I have friends, two or three,
Playing dolls and having fun.
Thelma is the extra one
Who is there when she should be
Somewhere else and not with me.

I have seen her several times
With an uncle who gives dimes
Going to the movies. They will take
Other friends, and they have cake
Topped with ice-cream after. All good chances
Go to other friends than Frances.

My friend Thelma is a pain but one that I can stay with.
I know people who have even worse than her to play with.

My First Love

MICHAEL ROSEN

A true story.

First love
when I was ten.

We planned a trip
up to town.
Quite a grand thing to do.
Up to town.
The long ride on the train
all the way
up to town.

The day before our trip
up to town
she said, 'Do you mind if Helen
comes with us
up to town?'
'Great,' I said,
'all three of us, we'll all go
on the train
up to town.'

So that's how it was—
all three of us,
her, Helen, and me
going on our trip
up to town.

But when we got
up to town,
all three of us—
her, Helen, and me,

there was this long tunnel
and her friend, Helen,
goes and says:
'Hey—let's run away from him.'
And that's what they did.

So then there wasn't
all three of us any more.
There was just me,
standing in the tunnel.
I didn't chase after them.
I went home.

Sally

PHOEBE HESKETH

She was a dog-rose kind of girl:
elusive, scattery as petals;
scratchy sometimes, tripping you like briars.
She teased the boys
turning this way and that, not to be tamed
or taught any more than the wind.
Even in school the word 'ought'
had no meaning for Sally.
On dull days
she'd sit quiet as a mole at her desk
delving in thought.
But when the sun called
she was gone, running the blue day down
till the warm hedgerows prickled the dusk
and moths flickered out.

Her mother scolded; Dad
gave her the hazel-switch,
said her head was stuffed with feathers
and a starling tongue.
But they couldn't take the shine out of her.
Even when it rained
you felt the sun saved under her skin.
She'd a way of escape
laughing at you from the bright end of a tunnel,
leaving you in the dark.

My Life
JULIE O'CALLAGHAN

Look at it coming
down the street
toward us:
it chokes me up
every time I see it
walking along
all by itself.
How does it know
for example
which corner
is the right one
to turn at?
Who tells it
to keep going
past the intersection
and take the first left
after the supermarket?
There it goes—
I'll follow quietly
and see where
it's off to.

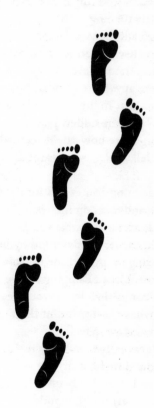

Child Wondering

ROY FULLER

I wonder what I used to be
Before I started out as me.
I remember crawling on the floor
But hardly anything before.
Yet sometimes waking in the dark
I see a little turning spark
As though another world had once
Impressed itself upon my glance;
And hear a train I never hear
In daytime anywhere so near;
And think that in the whole of space
To be in bed's the oddest place,
Forgetting quite how safe it seemed
Before I fell asleep and dreamed.

When morning comes and sunlight falls
On maps and faces on the walls,
And birds are saying what can be
Hummed but not understood by me;
And reading in my bedside books
Of pies made out of singing rooks,
And the complaints by nervous bears
Of girls whose bottoms dint their chairs—
Gradually I start to feel
The realness of the strangely real;
And by the time I cut my bacon
Know that I'm probably mistaken
To think it's any use to wonder
What lies behind, in front, out yonder.

One
JAMES BERRY

Only one of me
and nobody can get a second one
from a photocopy machine.

Nobody has the fingerprints I have.
Nobody can cry my tears, or laugh my laugh
or have my expectancy when I wait.

But anybody can mimic my dance with my dog.
Anybody can howl how I sing out of tune.
And mirrors can show me multiplied
many times, say, dressed up in red
or dressed up in grey.

Nobody can get into my clothes for me
or feel my fall for me, or do my running.
Nobody hears my music for me, either.

I am just this one.
Nobody else makes the words
I shape with sound, when I talk.

But anybody can act how I stutter in a rage.
Anybody can copy echoes I make.
And mirrors can show me multiplied
many times, say, dressed up in green
or dressed up in blue.

Montana Born

LEONARD CLARK

I saw her first through wavering candlelight,
My sister in her cradle, one hour old;
Outside, the snow was drifting through the night,
But she lay warm, oblivious to the cold.

Her eyes were closed, the half-moist wisps of hair,
A honey harvest on her wrinkled head,
The smile upon her face as if she was elsewhere,
But knew the land she had inherited.

My mother there at peace, her labour done,
Their greyness gone, her cheeks were coralline,
She welcomed me, her wondering first-born son
And placed my sister's new-nailed hand in mine.

I looked through the freezing window pane,
The whitening acre bare and stretching far
That nine months hence would heave with swelling grain,
And over every distant peak a star.

And she, my winter sister, does she know
That all this homely countryside is hers,
Where once were warring Sioux and buffalo,
And covered waggons full of travellers?

But I will tell her the Indian tales,
And show her grass-high fields, and sugar beet,
We'll ride all day along the western trails,
Missouri River glinting at our feet.

Montana born, she'll sleep beneath these beams,
And learn the simple ways, and say her prayers,
And even now she may see in her dreams
Another boy come climbing up the stairs.

I'm Not Old Enough Yet

JACKIE KAY

Even at three, this business of a big man
coming down the chimney loaded with pressies
from your list (who showed it to him?
Why wasn't he covered in soot?) seemed a bit far-fetched.
Especially since we didn't have a chimney.
But later I started to believe in this man
with the beard longer than God's.
I left food out. I tried to stay awake.
I still suspected Santa was a black woman dressed in red,
but I never, since three, asked my mum any questions.
Now I'm seven. A pal of mine asks, 'Do you believe
in Santa Claus?' *What do you mean?* 'Do you think it's true,'
she continued until my mouth fell open and I started to scream:
You shouldn't have told me. I'm not old enough yet.

To Our Daughter
JENNIFER ARMITAGE

And she is beautiful, our daughter.
Only six months, but a person.
She turns to look at everything, out walking.
All so precious. I mustn't disturb it with words.
People are like great clowns,
Blossom like balloons, black pigeons like eagles,
Water beyond belief.

She holds out her hand to air,
Sea, sky, wind, sun, movement, stillness,
And wants to hold them all.
My finger is her earth connection, me, and earth.

Her head is like an apple, or an egg.
Skin stretched fine over a strong casing.
Her whole being developing from within
And from without: the answer.

And she sings, long notes from the belly or the throat,
Her legs kick her feet up to her nose,
She rests—laid still like a large rose.
She is our child,
The world is not hers, she has to win it.

For the Child Who Became Christopher
ROBERT HULL

May you come safe
    and flawless

May they gaze in awe
    at your small creased wrists
        and marvel
            at your perfect breath
                and ordinariness

May they gurgle at you
    and drool gratitude

May your gaze and grip
    reassure them

May your limbs
    be proper and deft
        your crawl furious
            your falls neat

May your most frightening dark
        be in stories
    the deepest thunder
        over the hills yonder

May no one fence you round
    with their own hopes
        or shawl you in their dreams

May your teachers learn
    from your crazes
        and amazements

May your friends
    be a bridge to cross over
        in any weather

May you have without too much wanting
    and want without too much need

May there be sacred places
    to return to

May stones fall short
    and only low branches break
        and swings miss you
            on the way back.

People
CHARLOTTE ZOLOTOW

Some people talk and talk
and never say a thing.
Some people look at you
and birds begin to sing.

Some people laugh and laugh
and yet you want to cry.
Some people touch your hand
and music fills the sky.

People
D. H. LAWRENCE

I like people quite well
at a little distance.
I like to see them passing and passing
and going their own way,
especially if I see their aloneness alive in them.
Yet I don't want them to come near.
If they will only leave me alone
I can still have the illusion that there is room
  enough in the world.

The Salesman

JOHN FENNIMAN

There's this ring at the door and God,
surprised, goes and opens it, and sees
a bright young angel, case in hand
and smile on face: 'Good morning, Sir.
Is Madam in? No? Then perhaps I can
interest you?' And opens up his case.
At first there's nothing, a darkness so
intense God feels he's falling into it.
'I've also got . . .' the salesman says, sharp
and quick, and flips aside the dark
and, lying under, separate, a light
brighter than ten thousand suns.
'Well, yes', says God, a plan forming.
The deal is done; the angel gone: day one.

I expect you guess: it's every day
the doorbell rings: same smile, same case,
but inside, always something new:
a green-heaving sea with salt-spray tang;
a flash of fish, an exultation of larks,
a shade of woodland, a dazzle of mountain peaks,
a leap of leopards, an ostentation of peacocks.
Through five days God builds his Eden.
Day six: he's by the door, impatient,
what greater wonder can yet come?
Two naked figures: Adam, Eve.
'That's it', the salesman says. 'I'll not be back.
You'll need a rest tomorrow. I warn you now
these two are trouble'. And we are.

The Sound Collector

ROGER McGOUGH

A stranger called this morning
Dressed all in black and grey
Put every sound into a bag
And carried them away.

The whistling of the kettle
The turning of the lock
The purring of the kitten
The ticking of the clock

The popping of the toaster
The crunching of the flakes
When you spread the marmalade
The scraping noise it makes

The hissing of the frying-pan
The ticking of the grill
The bubbling of the bathtub
As it starts to fill

The drumming of the raindrops
On the window-pane
When you do the washing-up
The gurgle of the drain

The crying of the baby
The squeaking of the chair
The swishing of the curtain
The creaking of the stair

A stranger called this morning
He didn't leave his name
Left us only silence
Life will never be the same.

Mrs Murphy and Mrs Murphy's Kids

DENNIS LEE

Mrs Murphy,
　　If you please,
Kept her kids
　　In a can of peas.
The kids got bigger,
　　And the can filled up,
So she moved them into
　　A measuring cup.

But the kids got bigger
　　And the cup got crammed,
So she poured them into
　　A frying pan.
But the kids grew bigger
　　And the pan began to stink,
So she pitched them all
　　In the kitchen sink.

But the kids kept growing
　　And the sink went *kaplooey*,
So she dumped them on their ears
　　In a crate of chop suey.
But the kids kept growing
　　And the crate got stuck,
So she carted them away
　　In a ten-ton truck.

And she said, 'Thank goodness
　　I remembered that truck
Or my poor little children
　　Would be out of luck!'

But the darn kids grew
    Till the truck wouldn't fit,
And she had to haul them off
    To a gravel pit.

But the kids kept growing
    Till the pit was too small,
So she bedded them down
    In a shopping mall.
But the kids grew enormous
    And the mall wouldn't do,
So she herded them together
    In an empty zoo.

But the kids grew gigantic
    And the fence went *pop*!
So she towed them away
    To a mountain top.
But the kids just grew
    And the mountain broke apart,
And she said, 'Darned kids,
    They were pesky from the start!'

So she waited for a year,
    And she waited for another,
And the kids grew up
    And had babies like their mother.
And Mrs Murphy's kids—
    You can think what you please—
Kept all *their* kids
    In a can of peas.

The Dirtiest Man in the World

SHEL SILVERSTEIN

Oh I'm Dirty Dan, the world's dirtiest man,
I never have taken a shower.
I can't see my shirt—it's so covered with dirt,
And my ears have enough to grow flowers.

But the water is either a little too hot,
Or else it's a little too cold.
I'm musty and dusty and patchy and scratchy
And mangy and covered with mold.
But the water is always a little too hot,
Or else it's a little too cold.

I live in a pen with five hogs and a hen
And three squizzly lizards who creep in
My bed, and they itch as I squirm, and I twitch
In the cruddy old sheets that I sleep in.

If you looked down my throat with a flashlight, you'd note
That my insides are coated with rust.
I creak when I walk and I squeak when I talk,
And each time I sneeze I blow dust.

The thought of a towel and some soap makes me howl,
And when people have something to tell me
They don't come and tell it—they stand back and yell it.
I think they're afraid they might smell me.

The bedbugs that leap on me sing me to sleep,
And the garbage flies buzz me awake.
They're the best friends I've found and I fear they might drown
So I never go too near a lake.

Each evening at nine I sit down to dine
With the termites who live in my chair,
And I joke with the bats and have intimate chats
With the cooties who crawl through my hair.

I'd brighten my life if I just found a wife,
But I fear that that never will be
Until I can find a girl, gentle and kind,
With a beautiful face and a sensitive mind,
Who sparkles and twinkles and glistens and shines—
And who's almost as dirty as me.

Mrs Lorris, Who Died of Being Clean

BARBARA GILES

Mrs Lorris was a fusser
always asking, 'Is it clean?'
boiled her knives and forks twice daily,
vacuumed the village green.
When she took the bus to market
she spread a towel on the seat,
washed her hands in disinfectant
before sitting down to eat.
She never ate raw food like lettuce—
'Full of germs,' she used to say
and by her strenuous housecleaning
hoped to keep the germs away.
Always at it, night and morning,
with the scrubbing-brush and soap—
still she wasn't really certain
so she bought a microscope.
Horrid horror, in the eyepiece
microbes swarmed on every side:
too much for Mrs Lorris, who
pegged her nostrils up and died.

You are Old, Father William

LEWIS CARROLL

'You are old, Father William,' the young man said,
   'And your hair has become very white;
And yet you incessantly stand on your head—
   Do you think, at your age, it is right?'

'In my youth,' Father William replied to his son,
   'I feared it might injure the brain;
But now that I'm perfectly sure I have none,
   Why, I do it again and again.'

'You are old,' said the youth, 'as I mentioned before,
   And have grown most uncommonly fat;
Yet you turned a back-somersault in at the door—
   Pray, what is the reason of that?'

'In my youth,' said the sage, as he shook his grey locks,
   'I kept all my limbs very supple
By the use of this ointment—one shilling the box—
   Allow me to sell you a couple.'

'You are old,' said the youth, 'and your jaws are too weak
   For anything tougher than suet;
Yet you finished the goose, with the bones and the beak—
   Pray, how did you manage to do it?'

'In my youth,' said his father, 'I took to the law,
   And argued each case with my wife;
And the muscular strength which it gave to my jaw
   Has lasted the rest of my life.'

'You are old,' said the youth; 'one would hardly suppose
    That your eye was as steady as ever;
Yet you balanced an eel on the end of your nose—
    What made you so awfully clever?'

'I have answered three questions, and that is enough,'
    Said his father; 'don't give yourself airs!
Do you think I can listen all day to such stuff?
    Be off, or I'll kick you down stairs!'

The Birderman
ROGER McGOUGH

Most weekends, starting in the spring
Until late summer, I spend angling.
Not for fish. I find that far too tame
But for birds, a much more interesting game.

A juicy worm I use as bait
Cast a line into the tree and wait.
Seldom for long (that's half the fun)
A commotion in the leaves, the job's half done.

Pull hard, jerk home the hook
Then reel him in. Let's have a look . . .
A tiny thing, a fledgling, young enough to spare.
I show mercy. Unhook, and toss it to the air.

It flies nestwards and disappears among the leaves
(What man roasts and braises, he too reprieves).
What next? A magpie. Note the splendid tail.
I wring its neck. Though stringy, it'll pass for quail.

Unlike water, the depths of trees are high
So, standing back, I cast into the sky.
And ledger there beyond the topmost bough,
Until threshing down, like a black cape, screams a crow.

Evil creature! A witch in feathered form.
I try to net the dark, encircling storm.
It caws for help. Its cronies gather round
They curse and swoop. I hold my ground.

An infernal mass, a black, horrific army
I'll not succumb to Satan's origami.
I reach into my coat, I've come prepared,
Bring out my pocket scarecrow—Watch out, bird!

It's cross-shaped, the sign the godless fear
In a thunderflap of wings they disappear.
Except of course, that one, ungainly kite
Broken now, and quickly losing height.

I haul it in, and with a single blow
Dispatch it to that Aviary below.
The ebb and flow: magpie, thrush, nightingale, and crow.
The wood darkens. Time to go.

I pack away the food I've caught
And thankful for a good day's sport
Amble home. The forest fisherman.
And I'll return as soon as I can

To bird. For I'm a birderer. The birderman.

The Woman and the Knife-Thrower

ROSITA BOLAND

I am the woman whom the knife-thrower
Redefines each night,
The knives flying surely
From his calloused palm.

I have no beauty, no humour,
No lithe and acrobatic skills
And so I have become a human prop
In this tawdry circus.

The knife-thrower
Knows the outlines of my body
As no other person does.

All day, he sits on the caravan steps
And polishes knives.
He watches me
In the reflection of their cruel blades.

Night after night,
I entrust my body to him.

We mark each other, eye to eye,
And the knives come like the words
He will never speak.

They brush against my flesh, glittering
With the brightness of unshed tears.

Eddie Don't Like Furniture

JOHN HEGLEY

Eddie don't go for sofas or settees
or those little tables that you have to buy in threes
the closest thing that Eddie's got to an article of furniture's
the cheese board
Eddie doesn't bolster the upholstery biz
there's a lot of furniture in the world but none of it's Eddie's
he won't have it in the house however well it's made
Eddie's bedroom was fully furnished
when the floorboards had been laid
and Eddie played guitar
until he decided that his guitar was far too like
an article of furniture
Eddie offers visitors a corner of the room
you get used to the distances between you pretty soon
but with everyone in corners though
it isn't very easy when you're trying to play pontoon
he once got in a rowing boat and they offered him a seat

it was just a strip of timber but it wasn't up his street
he stood himself up in the boat and made himself feel steady
then he threw the plank onto the bank and said
furniture?
no thank you
when it's on a bonfire furniture's fine
any time that Eddie gets a number twenty-nine bus
even if there's seats on top and plenty down below
Eddie always goes where the pushchairs go
does Eddie like furniture?
I don't think so
if you go round Eddie's place and have a game of hide and seek
it isn't very long before you're found
and in a fit of craziness Eddie took the legs off his dash hound
that stopped him dashing around
Eddie quite likes cutlery
but he don't like furniture
if you give him some for Christmas
he'll returniture

The Gardener

ANON.

The gardener stood at the garden gate,
   A primrose in his hand;
He saw a lovely girl come by,
   Slim as a willow wand.

'O lady, can you fancy me,
   And will you share my life?
All my garden flowers are yours,
   If you will be my wife.

'The white lily will be your shirt
   It suits your body best;
With cornflowers in your hair,
   A red rose on your breast.

'Your gloves will be the marigold,
   Glittering on your hand;
Your dress will be the sweet-william
   That grows upon the bank.'

'Young man, I cannot be your wife;
   I fear it will not do.
Although you care for me,' she said,
   'I cannot care for you.

'As you've provided clothes for me
   Among the summer flowers,
So I'll provide some clothes for you
   Among the winter showers.

'The fallen snow will be your shirt,
　　It suits your body best;
Your head will be wound with the eastern wind,
　　With the cold rain on your breast.

'Your boots will be of the seaweed
　　That drifts upon the tide;
Your horse will be the white wave—
　　Leap on, young man, and ride!'

Lochinvar

SIR WALTER SCOTT

O young Lochinvar is come out of the west,
Through all the wide Border his steed was the best;
And save his good broadsword he weapons had none,
He rode all unarm'd, and he rode all alone.
So faithful in love, and so dauntless in war,
There never was knight like the young Lochinvar.

He staid not for brake, and he stopp'd not for stone,
He swam the Eske river where ford there was none;
But ere he alighted at Netherby gate,
The bride had consented, the gallant came late:
For a laggard in love, and a dastard in war,
Was to wed the fair Ellen of brave Lochinvar.

So boldly he enter'd the Netherby Hall,
Among bride's-men, and kinsmen, and brothers, and all:
Then spoke the bride's father, his hand on his sword,
(For the poor craven bridegroom said never a word,)
'O come ye in peace here, or come ye in war,
Or to dance at our bridal, young Lord Lochinvar?'

'I long woo'd your daughter, my suit you denied;—
Love swells like the Solway, but ebbs like its tide—
And now am I come, with this lost love of mine
To lead but one measure, drink one cup of wine.
There are maidens in Scotland more lovely by far,
That would gladly be bride to the young Lochinvar.'

The bride kiss'd the goblet: the knight took it up,
He quaff'd off the wine, and he threw down the cup.
She look'd down to blush, and she look'd up to sigh,
With a smile on her lips, and a tear in her eye.
He took her soft hand, ere her mother could bar,—
'Now tread we a measure!' said young Lochinvar.

So stately his form, and so lovely her face,
That never a hall such a galliard did grace;
While her mother did fret, and her father did fume,
And the bridegroom stood dangling his bonnet and plume;
And the bride-maidens whisper'd, ''Twere better by far
To have match'd our fair cousin with young Lochinvar.'

One touch to her hand, and one word in her ear,
When they reach'd the hall-door, and the charger stood near;
So light to the croupe the fair lady he swung,
So light to the saddle before her he sprung!
'She is won! we are gone, over bank, bush, and scaur;
They'll have fleet steeds that follow,' quoth young Lochinvar.

There was mounting 'mong Graemes of the Netherby clan;
Forsters, Fenwicks, and Musgraves, they rode and they ran:
There was racing and chasing on Cannobie Lee,
But the lost bride of Netherby ne'er did they see.
So daring in love, and so dauntless in war,
Have ye e'er heard of gallant like young Lochinvar?

Work and Play

TED HUGHES

The swallow of summer, she toils all summer,
A blue-dark knot of glittering voltage,
A whiplash swimmer, a fish of the air.
But the serpent of cars that crawls through the dust
In shimmering exhaust
Searching to slake
Its fever in ocean
Will play and be idle or else it will bust.

The swallow of summer, the barbed harpoon,
She flings from the furnace, a rainbow of purples,
Dips her glow in the pond and is perfect.
But the serpent of cars that collapsed at the beach
Disgorges its organs
A scamper of colours
Which roll like tomatoes
Nude as tomatoes
With sand in their creases
To cringe in the sparkle of rollers and screech.

The swallow of summer, the seamstress of summer,
She scissors the blue into shapes and she sews it,
She draws a long thread and she knots it at corners.
But the holiday people
Are laid out like wounded
Flat as in ovens
Roasting and basting
With faces of torment as space burns them blue
Their heads are transistors
Their teeth grit on sand grains
Their lost kids are squalling

While man-eating flies
Jab electric shock needles but what can they do?

They can climb in their cars with raw bodies, raw faces
    And start up the serpent
    And headache it homeward
    A car full of squabbles
    And sobbing and stickiness
    With sand in their crannies
    Inhaling petroleum
    That pours from the foxgloves
    While the evening swallow
The swallow of summer, cartwheeling through crimson,
Touches the honey-slow river and turning
Returns to the hand stretched from under the eaves—
A boomerang of rejoicing shadow.

People-in-Cars

PHILIP GROSS

People-in-cars are ugly.
The big ones sag baggy as toads.
The small ones sit up smugly
   like prize porkers on their way to market.

People-in-cars ignore
the rest of us. We're a boring old film
they've seen before
   and can change with a flick of the gearstick.

People-in-cars are gross.
They have horns and are noisy and deaf.
At traffic lights they pick their noses
   and sing with their stereos, flat.

Young people-in-cars demand
things with menaces: sweets and crisps
and double jumbo burgers *and*
   an extra-thick milkshake. Then they're sick.

Parent people-in-cars go stiff
and turn their backs and drive,
drive, drive as if
   by going faster they might just escape.

They're all monsters, half human, half car.
They go in herds and hate
each other. This has gone too far.
   The time has come to say it straight:
   there ought to be a law against them stamp them out clamp
      down exterminate exterminate ...

   (*Other* people in cars, that is.)

My busconductor

ROGER McGOUGH

My busconductor tells me
he only has one kidney
and that may soon go on strike
through overwork.
Each busticket
takes on a different shape
and texture.
He holds a ninepenny single
as if it were a rose
and puts the shilling in his bag
as a child into a gasmeter.

His thin lips
have no quips
for fat factorygirls
and he ignores
the drunk who snores
and the oldman who talks to himself
and gets off at the wrong stop.
He goes gently to the bedroom
of the bus
to collect
and watch familiar shops and pubs passby
(perhaps for the last time?)
The sameold streets look different now
more distinct
as through new glasses.
And the sky
was it ever so blue?

And all the time
deepdown in the deserted busshelter of his mind
he thinks about his journey nearly done.
One day he'll clock on and never clock off
or clock off and never clock on.

The City People Meet Themselves

ROSANNE FLYNN

The city people meet themselves
as they stare in the mirror of the opposite seat.
An old woman smiles at her reflection—
a girl, who's late for work
and urges the train on with a tapping foot—
the crumpled old woman remembers when
her feet tapped to speed up life
but now the feet are tired and old
and each step aches with dwindling hours:
a starched commuter tries not to look
at the broken-down man who cries—
his shallow eyes, pools of hopelessness,
the business man prays that life will be kind
and the treadmill of time will not leave him to cry
in the loneliness of a busy train;
an eager boy gapes at his reflection,
a huge man whose long arms reach to the straps
and smothers the boy in an aura of greatness—
the boy longs for the distant time
when his arms will reach
into the unknown realms of adulthood;
a worn out mother stares across
and sees another woman with the same gaze
grateful for child, but mournful for freedom.
Their eyes meet in silent conversation.

Long, Long Ago

ALDEN NOWLAN

It seems I always saw the Indian woman
the instant she became visible,
and never took my eyes off her
as she lugged her many-coloured pack,
three times as big as herself,
down South Mountain,
across Little Bridge,
up North Mountain
and into our kitchen
where she undid a knot
and flooded the entire room with baskets
—cherry-coloured baskets,
wheat-coloured baskets,
cabbage-coloured baskets,
baskets the colour of a November sky,
each basket containing
another, smaller basket,
down to one so tiny it would hold
only a hang of thread and a thimble.

All the Dogs

MATTHEW SWEENEY

You should have seen him—
he stood in the park and whistled,
underneath an oak tree,
and all the dogs came bounding up
and sat around him,
keeping their big eyes on him,
tails going like pendulums.
And there was one cocker pup
who went and licked his hand,
and a Labrador who whimpered
till the rest joined in.

Then he whistled a second time,
high-pitched as a stoat,
over all the shouted dog names
and whistles of owners,
till a flurry of paws
brought more dogs, panting,
as if they'd come miles,
and these too found space
on the flattened grass
to stare at the boy's
unmemorable face
which all the dogs found special.

Watching a Dancer

JAMES BERRY

She wears a red costume for her dance.
Her body is trim
and shapely and strong.

Before she begins
she waits composed,
waiting to hear the music start.

The music moves her.
She hears it keenly. The music
pulses her body with its rhythms.

It delights her. It haunts her body
into patterns of curves and angles.
She rocks. She spins.

She stretches entranced. She looks
she could swim and could fly.
She would stay airborne from a leap.

Her busy head, arms, legs, all know
she shows how the music looks.
Posture changes and movements are

the language of the sounds, that
she and the music use together
and reveal their unfolding story.

The Busker

GERARD BENSON

His elbow jerks, an old mechanical toy.
Feet planted astride, knees flexed, one instep
Arched over the cobbles, he scratches a tune
From a bony violin, grating the spine.

His left hand, a dancing spider, performs
Its polka on the taut web strings, his right,
Daintier than a lady taking tea,
Guides the thin bow in dangerous little stabs,

Littering the yard with snips and snaps of sound,
Sharper than pins. Coins drop into his hat,
But sparingly, and pigeons on pink unhurried feet
Waddle, chatting by; refuse, point-blank, to dance.

Refugees

VERNON SCANNELL

In dusk of helmet-brims the eyes look stern,
Unwavering, no matter what they see
Or where they gaze—Bluff Cove, Thermopylae,
Kuwait, the Somme. The pillaged cities burn,
And when the owners of those eyes return
And put away their weapons there will be
An alien music in a harsher key,
New words and syntax difficult to learn.
Wars never end. Across the livid plain
The dark processions trail, the refugees,
Anonymous beneath indifferent skies,
Somnambulistic, patient shapes of pain,
Long commentary on war, an ancient frieze
Of figures we refuse to recognize.

Say this City has Ten Million Souls

W. H. AUDEN

Say this city has ten million souls,
Some are living in mansions, some are living in holes:
Yet there's no place for us, my dear, yet there's no place for us.

Once we had a country and we thought it fair,
Look in the atlas and you'll find it there:
We cannot go there now, my dear, we cannot go there now.

In the village churchyard there grows an old yew,
Every spring it blossoms anew:
Old passports can't do that, my dear, old passports can't do that.

The consul banged the table and said;
'If you've got no passport you're officially dead':
But we are still alive, my dear, but we are still alive.

Went to a committee; they offered me a chair;
Asked me politely to return next year:
But where shall we go today, my dear, but where shall we go
    today?

Came to a public meeting; the speaker got up and said:
'If we let them in, they will steal our daily bread';
He was talking of you and me, my dear, he was talking of you
    and me.

Thought I heard the thunder rumbling in the sky;
It was Hitler over Europe, saying: 'They must die';
O we were in his mind, my dear, O we were in his mind.

Saw a poodle in a jacket fastened with a pin,
Saw a door opened and a cat let in:
But they weren't German Jews, my dear, but they weren't
 German Jews.

Went down the harbour and stood upon the quay,
Saw the fish swimming as if they were free:
Only ten feet away, my dear, only ten feet away.

Walked through a wood, saw the birds in the trees;
They had no politicians and sang at their ease:
They weren't the human race, my dear, they weren't the
 human race.

Dreamed I saw a building with a thousand floors,
A thousand windows and a thousand doors;
Not one of them was ours, my dear, not one of them was ours.

Stood on a great plain in the falling snow;
Ten thousand soldiers marched to and fro:
Looking for you and me, my dear, looking for you and me.

But No One Cares

ANON.

The day was long.
The winds blew on
But no one cared.

All alone,
Had no home,
But no one cared.

He fought against the wind and rain
Although he had a lot of pain,
But no one cared.

The day grew old
The night was cold
But no one cared.

The stars above
Were his only love
He left no mark
But no one cared.

He had feelings
Of his piteous meanings
But no one cared.

In the still of the night
He felt unright
But no one cared.

He could have died,
Instead he cried,
But no one cared.

Anorexic

GILLIAN CLARKE

My father's sister,
the one who died
before there was a word for it,
was fussy with her food.
'Eat up', they'd say to me,
ladling a bowl with warning.

What I remember's
how she'd send me to the dairy,
taught to take cream,
the standing gold.
Where the jug dipped
I saw its blue-milk skin
before the surface healed.

Breath held, tongue between teeth,
I carried in the cream,
brimmed, level,
parallel, I knew,
with that other, hidden horizon
of the earth's deep
ungleaming water-table.

And she, more often than not half-dressed,
stockings, a slip, a Chinese kimono,
would warm that cream, pour it
with crumbled melting cheese
over a delicate white cauliflower,
or field mushrooms
steaming in porcelain,
then watch us eat, relishing,
smoking her umpteenth cigarette,
glamorous, perfumed, starved,
and going to die.

The Chinese Checker Players

RICHARD BRAUTIGAN

When I was six years old
I played Chinese checkers
 with a woman
who was ninety-three years old.
She lived by herself
in an apartment down the hall
 from ours.
We played Chinese checkers
every Monday and Thursday nights.
While we played she usually talked
about her husband
who had been dead for seventy years,
and we drank tea and ate cookies
 and cheated.

Ideal Gnome

ADRIAN HENRI

An old gnome sat
in an Old Gnome's Home
and talked of gardens he had known;
he sat and talked of days gone by,
of fish and frogs and dragonfly,
remembering the willowtree, the rockery
where he had stood for years and fished.
As his eyes filled with tears, he wished
that he could go back to the place
he used to know, that's now
a concrete patio. Sometimes he just sits
and dreams about the day they came
with the machines, pulled up the tree,
and poured the concrete on.
Now it's all gone.
    The Gnome's Home's
an ideal home for one old gnome
who talks of better days he's seen.
With misted eyes he sees the green weed,
watches the goldfish rise.

PC Plod versus the Dale St. Dog Strangler

ROGER McGOUGH

For several months
Liverpool was held in the grip of fear
by a dogstrangler most devilish,
who roamed the streets after dark
looking for strays. Finding one
he would tickle it seductively
about the body to gain its confidence,
then lead it down a deserted backstreet
where he would strangle the poor brute.
Hardly a night passed without somebody's
faithful fourlegged friend being dispatched
to that Golden Kennel in the sky.

> *The public were warned,*
> *At the very first sign*
> *of anything suspicious*
> *ring Canine-nine-nine.*

Nine o'clock on the evening of January 11th
sees PC Plod on the corner
of Dale Street and Sir Thomas Street
disguised as a Welsh collie.
It is part of a daring plan to apprehend the strangler.
For though it is a wet and moonless night,
Plod is cheered in the knowledge
that the whole of the Liverpool City Constabulary
is on the beat that night disguised as dogs.
Not ten minutes earlier, a pekinese
(Policewoman Hodges)

had scampered past on her way to Clayton Square.
For Plod, the night passed uneventfully
and so in the morning he was horrified to learn
that no less than fourteen policemen and policewomen
had been tickled and strangled during the night.

The public were horrified
The Commissioner aghast
Something had to be done
And fast.

PC Plod (wise as a brace of owls)
met the challenge magnificently
and submitted an idea so startling in its vision
so audacious in its conception
that the Commissioner gasped
before ordering all dogs in the city
to be thereinafter disguised as fuzz.
The plan worked
and the dogstrangler was heard of no more.

Cops and mongrels
like PCs in a pod
To a grateful public
Plod was God.

So next time you're up in Liverpool
take a closer look
at that policeman on pointduty
he might well be a copper spaniel.

Stealing

CAROL ANN DUFFY

The most unusual thing I ever stole? A snowman.
Midnight. He looked magnificent; a tall, white mute
beneath the winter moon. I wanted him, a mate
with a mind as cold as the slice of ice
within my own brain. I started with the head.

Better off dead than giving in, not taking
what you want. He weighed a ton; his torso,
frozen stiff, hugged to my chest, a fierce chill
piercing my gut. Part of the thrill was knowing
that children would cry in the morning. Life's tough.

Sometimes I steal things I don't need. I joy-ride cars
to nowhere, break into houses just to have a look.
I'm a mucky ghost, leave a mess, maybe pinch a camera.
I watch my gloved hand twisting the doorknob.
A stranger's bedroom. Mirrors. I sigh like this—*Aah.*

It took some time. Reassembled in the yard,
he didn't look the same. I took a run
and booted him. Again. Again. My breath ripped out
in rags. It seems daft now. Then I was standing
alone amongst lumps of snow, sick of the world.

Boredom. Mostly I'm so bored I could eat myself.
One time, I stole a guitar and thought I might
learn to play. I nicked a bust of Shakespeare once,
flogged it, but the snowman was strangest.
You don't understand a word I'm saying, do you?

The Death of a Scoutmaster

JOHN HEGLEY

how I remember the old scoutmaster
nobody could start a camp-fire faster
I can see the old scoutmaster in the old scout hut
saying always carry a plaster
in case you cut yourself
if it doesn't happen to you it could happen to your dog
you could be chopping up the firewood
when you mistake him for a log
if it doesn't happen to your dog
it could happen to your glasses
they could be knocked to the floor
by the long arm of the law
when you're standing on the corner
and a copper on a push-bike signalling a left turn passes by
if it's friend you need you need a friend indeed
you need a plaster
you need your money and your keys
but more than these you need a plaster
always carry a plaster our scoutmaster told us
they found one in his pocket
the day a bus ran over him

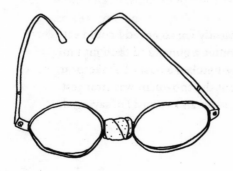

Willie

MAYA ANGELOU

Willie was a man without fame,
Hardly anybody knew his name.
Crippled and limping, always walking lame,
He said, 'I keep on movin'
Movin' just the same.'

Solitude was the climate in his head,
Emptiness was the partner in his bed,
Pain echoed in the steps of his tread,
He said, 'I keep on followin'
Where the leaders led.

'I may cry and I will die,
But my spirit is the soul of every spring,
Watch for me and you will see
That I'm present in the songs that children sing.'

People called him 'Uncle', 'Boy', and 'Hey',
Said, 'You can't live through this another day.'
Then, they waited to hear what he would say.
He said, 'I'm living
In the games that children play.

'You may enter my sleep, people my dreams,
Threaten my early morning's ease,
But I keep comin' followin' laughin' cryin',
Sure as a summer breeze.

'Wait for me, watch for me.
My spirit is the surge of open seas.
Look for me, ask for me,
I'm the rustle in the autumn leaves.

'When the sun rises
I am the time.
When the children sing
I am the Rhyme.'

Not Waving but Drowning

STEVIE SMITH

Nobody heard him, the dead man,
But still he lay moaning:
I was much further out than you thought
And not waving but drowning.

Poor chap, he always loved larking
And now he's dead.
It must have been too cold for him his heart gave way,
They said.

Oh, no no no, it was too cold always
(Still the dead one lay moaning)
I was much too far out all my life
And not waving but drowning.

Dirge for Unwin

PHILIP GROSS

Uncle Unwin
lived unwed,
died unmourned,
our tears unshed,
his chin unshaved,
his soul unsaved,
his feet unwashed,
his cat unfed,

uncouth, unkempt,
no cuff unfrayed,
his floor unswept,
his bed unmade,
ungenerous,
unkind to us,
the undertaker's
bill unpaid

until
    his will,
found undercover,
left untold wealth
to an unknown lover.
It's so unfair.
We were unaware:
even nobodies count
on one another.

Epitaph for Mary Bond

Here lie the bodies
Of THOMAS BOND, and MARY his wife.
She was temperate, chaste, charitable,
BUT
She was proud, peevish, and passionate.
She was an affectionate wife, and a tender mother;
BUT
Her husband and child, whom she loved,
Seldom saw her countenance without a disgusting frown;
Whilst she received visitors, whom she despised,
With an endearing smile.
Her behaviour was discreet towards strangers,
BUT
Imprudent in her family.
Abroad, her conduct was influenced by good breeding
BUT
At home by ill temper.
She was a professed enemy to flattery,
And was seldom known to praise or commend;
BUT
The talents in which she principally excelled,
Were difference of opinion, and
Discovering flaws and imperfections.
She was an admirable economist,
And, without prodigality,
Dispensed plenty to every person in her family;
BUT
Would sacrifice their eyes to a farthing candle.
She sometimes made her husband happy
With her good qualities;
BUT
Much more frequently miserable,

With her many failings;
Insomuch, that in thirty years cohabitation,
He often lamented,
That maugre all her virtues
He had not, in the whole, enjoyed
Two years of matrimonial comfort.
AT LENGTH,
Finding she had lost the affections of her husband,
As well as the regard of her neighbours,
Family disputes having been divulged by servants,
She died of vexation, July 20, 1768, aged 48.
Her worn-out husband survived her
Four months and two days,
And departed this life, Nov. 28, 1768, aged 54.
WILLIAM BOND, brother to the deceased,
Erected this stone,
As a weekly monitor to the surviving
Wives of this parish,
That they may avoid the infamy
Of having their memories handed down to posterity,
With a patchwork character.

ST JOHN, HORSLEYDOWN, BERMONDSEY, LONDON

Song

CHRISTINA ROSSETTI

When I am dead, my dearest,
   Sing no sad songs for me;
Plant thou no roses at my head,
   Nor shady cypress tree:
Be the green grass above me
   With showers and dewdrops wet;
And if thou wilt, remember,
   And if thou wilt, forget.
I shall not see the shadows,
   I shall not feel the rain;
I shall not hear the nightingale
   Sing on, as if in pain:
And dreaming through the twilight
   That doth not rise nor set,
Haply I may remember,
   And haply may forget.

Cowboy Song

CHARLES CAUSLEY

I come from Salem County
  Where the silver melons grow,
Where the wheat is sweet as an angel's feet
  And the zithering zephyrs blow.
I walk the blue bone-orchard
  In the apple-blossom snow,
When the teasy bees take their honeyed ease
  And the marmalade moon hangs low.

My Maw sleeps prone on the prairie
  In a boulder eiderdown,
Where the pickled stars in their little jam-jars
  Hang in a hoop to town.
I haven't seen Paw since a Sunday
  In eighteen seventy-three
When he packed his snap in a bitty mess-trap
  And said he'd be home by tea.

Fled is my fancy sister
  All weeping like the willow,
And dead is the brother I loved like no other
  Who once did share my pillow.
I fly the florid water
  Where run the seven geese round
O the townsfolk talk to see me walk
  Six inches off the ground.

Across the map of midnight
    I trawl the turning sky,
In my green glass the salt fleets pass
    The moon her fire-float by.
The girls go gay in the valley
    When the boys come down from the farm,
Don't run, my joy, from a poor cowboy,
    I won't do you no harm.

The bread of my twentieth birthday
    I buttered with the sun,
Though I sharpen my eyes with lovers' lies
    I'll never see twenty-one.
Light is my shirt with lilies,
    And lined with lead my hood,
On my face as I pass is a plate of brass,
    And my suit is made of wood.

The Doomed Spaceman

TED WALKER

I remember one winter-night meadow
Of sky-black grass
That lay beyond my childhood window
Of pearly glass
When I learned what it was to be lonely,
Packed off to bed
And lit by a glimmer that wanly
The frostfall shed.

The pane wiped clear, my crying over,
Darkness would yield
Its long cluster of summer-white clover
In a vast field;
Sleepless I stared for yearning hours,
And I began
Wanting to wander those infinite flowers
When a grown man.

And now I am lost in the heavens.
My meanderings
Further immeasurably flung than Saturn's
Exquisite rings
Into space that's unutterably lovely
With misted light
And every dusk is a dawn and every
Day is as night.
Straight my broken instruments steer:
I have no choice
But to bear silence in which I can hear
No human voice
Save mine at the capsule's clear window

When galaxies pass—
No dandelion Sun in no meadow
Of day-blue grass.

Weightless, helpless, I'm locked on a track
I can't reverse;
For one glimpse of home, I would give back
The universe.
Constellation by constellation
Like baby's breath
I journey through, my destination
Nowhere but Death.

Bedtime

JOHN FENNIMAN

Through shadows I climb the stairs
And think of those I used to know
Who lay down, once, and fled

Into the dark. They have gone,
Through the grave's narrow door,
Into that vast land of the dead.

I think of them as I lie still
And hear the voices in the house
That warm me as I lie safe in bed.

The Man Who Wasn't There

BRIAN LEE

Yesterday upon the stair
I met a man who wasn't there;
He wasn't there again today,
I wish, I wish, he'd go away.

I've seen his shapeless shadow-coat
Beneath the stairway, hanging about;
And outside, muffled in a cloak
The same colour as the dark;

I've seen him in a black, black suit
Shaking, under the broken light;
I've seen him swim across the floor
And disappear beneath the door;

And once, I almost heard his breath
Behind me, running up the path:
Inside, he leant against the wall,
And turned . . . and was no one at all.

Yesterday upon the stair
I met a man who wasn't there;
He wasn't there again today,
I wish, I wish, he'd go away.

In the Daytime

MICHAEL ROSEN

In the daytime I am Rob Roy and a tiger
In the daytime I am Marco Polo
               I chase bears in Bricket Wood
In the daytime I am the Tower of London
               nothing gets past me
               when it's my turn
               in Harrybo's hedge
In the daytime I am Henry the fifth and Ulysses
               and I tell stories
               that go on for a whole week
               if I want.
At night in the dark
               when I've shut the front room door
               I try and
               get up the stairs across the landing
               into bed and under the pillow
               without breathing once.

The Dark

ROY FULLER

I feared the darkness as a boy;
And if at night I had to go
Upstairs alone I'd make a show
Of carrying on with those below
A dialogue of shouts and 'whats?'
So they'd be sure to save poor Roy
Were he attacked by vampire bats.

Or thugs or ghosts. But far less crude
Than criminal or even ghost
Behind a curtain or a post
Was what I used to dread the most—
The always-unseen bugaboo
Of black-surrounded solitude.
I dread it still at sixty-two.

The Lurkers

ADRIAN HENRI

On our Estate
When it's getting late
In the middle of the night
They come in flocks
From beneath tower-blocks
And crawl towards the light

Down the Crescent
Up the Drive
Late at night
They come alive
Lurking here and lurking there
Sniffing at the midnight air

Up the Shopping Centre
You might just hear their call
Something like a bin-bag
Moving by the wall

Lurking at the bus-stop
Seen through broken glass
Something dark and slimy
Down the underpass

On our Estate
When it's getting late
In the middle of the night
There are things that lurk
About their work
Till dawn puts them to flight.

Multi Storey

PHILIP GROSS

'Level 13. Don't forget. By the car,'
   they said. 'Don't be late.'
      But you are.

You punch the buttons one by one.
   No hum. The lift is dead.
      So you run

up twist on twist of empty stair,
   can't stop, till the walls
      spin—bare

bone concrete splashed with beer
   or worse and spray-scrawls:
      WE WUZ ERE.

JEN 4 BAZ. Levels 8 . . . 9 . . . 10 . . .
   13 . . . Through the door, look.
      Look again:

it's wrong. Try one flight up. One more,
   up or down, no difference.
      Every floor,

it hits you with a breath of chill
   and stale fumes, is 13.
      And all so still.

The roof above, the floor beneath
   are closing on the light
     like teeth

as you hunt down line on silent line
   of cars like rusting waggons
     in a worked-out mine.

And inside every windscreen there are eyes
   as cold as mirrors, with a look
     you recognize

from Sunday snarl-ups queuing for the coast.
   They stare you back as if
     you were the ghost:

Dads grim as captains in the driving seat,
   Mums tight-lipped at their side.
     Their eyes never meet.

The back of their heads is all the kids see
   blocking out where they're going,
     that's patiently

waiting round the next bend out of sight
   as Dad puts his foot down. Squeal
     of brakes or fright

and *Wake up!* Just in time. These stories
   always end like that,
     don't they?
            Sure,
    all but one.

There Was a Naughty Boy

JOHN KEATS

There was a naughty boy,
  A naughty boy was he,
He would not stop at home,
  He could not quiet be—
      He took
      In his knapsack
      A book
      Full of vowels
      And a shirt
      With some towels,
      A slight cap
      For night cap,
      A hair brush,
      Comb ditto,
      New stockings—
      For old ones
      Would split O!
      This knapsack
      Tight at 's back
      He riveted close
And followed his nose
  To the North,
  To the North,
And followed his nose
  To the North.

There was a naughty boy,
   And a naughty boy was he,
He ran away to Scotland
   The people for to see—
      There he found
      That the ground
      Was as hard,
      That a yard
      Was as long,
      That a song
      Was as merry,
      That a cherry
      Was as red—
      That lead
      Was as weighty,
      That fourscore
      Was as eighty,
      That a door
      Was as wooden
      As in England—
So he stood in his shoes
   And he wondered,
   He wondered,
He stood in his shoes
   And he wondered.

Views from the Train

MICHAEL ROSEN

When you go on the train
and the line goes past the backs of houses
    in a town
you can see there's thousands and thousands
of things going on:
someone's washing up,
a baby's crying,
someone's shaving,
someone said, 'Rubbish, I blame
    the government.'
someone tickled a dog
someone looked out the window
and saw this train
and saw me looking at her
and she thought
'There's someone looking out the window
looking at me.'

But I'm only someone
looking out the window
looking at someone
looking out the window
looking at someone.

Then it's all gone.

Girl from a Train

GARETH OWEN

We stopped by a cornfield
Near Shrewsbury
A girl in a sun hat
Smiled at me.

Then I was seven
Now sixty-two
Wherever you are
I remember you.

Design

JULIE O'CALLAGHAN

I wanted to organize
my life into
a pattern.

Red socks and
a striped hairbow
on Wednesdays.

For a humdrum Tuesday,
spearmint gum
and a book about horses.

Saturdays, all I'd need
were tassels on my shoes
and a lace butterfly pin.

The way I felt
about Sunday
called for a white

linen dress and straw
hat, a story
about a river adventure.

Swinging

FRANK FLYNN

Whenever I feel a little bit sad
I go on the swings in our local park.
At first I move backwards and forwards
Ever so slow
Closely studying the floor as I go,
Watching its cracks and its stones
Like I'm on a spaceship
Flying ever so low.
After a minute or two of swinging
I don't feel half so bad
Perhaps it's because space pilots never appear sad.
I press the accelerator into top gear;
Launch myself up at the sky
Until I get so high
Down is the only place left to go.
I zoom earthward like a meteor
Heading down from the sun,
Swing high, Swing low,
When you're down on a swing
Up is the only way you can go,
Swing low, Swing high.

Cold Feet

BRIAN LEE

They have all gone across
They are all turning to see
They are all shouting 'come on'
They are all waiting for me.

I look through the gaps in the footway
And my heart shrivels with fear,
For far below the river is flowing
So quick and so cold and so clear.

And all that there is between it
And me falling down there is this:
A few wooden planks—not very thick—
And between each, a little abyss.

The holes get right under my sandals.
I can see straight through to the rocks,
And if I don't look, I can feel it,
Just there, through my shoes and my socks.

Suppose my feet and my legs withered up
And slipped through the slats like a rug?
Suppose I suddenly went very thin
Like the baby that slid down the plug?

I know that it cannot happen
But suppose that it did, what then?
Would they be able to find me
And take me back home again?

They have all gone across
They are all waiting to see
They are all shouting 'come on'—
But they'll have to carry me.

Torches

JOHN COTTON

It is the torches I remember best.
Going home on a winter's evening
We would point them skyward,
Screwing the fronts to sharpen the pencils of light
That they might pierce the darkness the better.
Bold young challengers of stars,
We competed in length and brightness.
Yes, better than the chips,
Tart with vinegar and salt grains,
In bags like small grease-proof hats,
Better even than the large orange bottles,
Tizer tasting of fruit that never was,
Were the torches,
Their beams like friendly knives
Making cuts in a darkness
Which oh so quickly healed
At the touch of a switch.

Who?

CHARLES CAUSLEY

Who is that child I see wandering, wandering
Down by the side of the quivering stream?
Why does he seem not to hear, though I call to him?
Where does he come from, and what is his name?

Why do I see him at sunrise and sunset
Taking, in old-fashioned clothes, the same track?
Why, when he walks, does he cast not a shadow
Though the sun rises and falls at his back?

Why does the dust lie so thick on the hedgerow
By the great field where a horse pulls the plough?
Why do I see only meadows, where houses
Stand in a line by the riverside now?

Why does he move like a wraith by the water,
Soft as the thistledown on the breeze blown?
When I draw near him so that I may hear him,
Why does he say that his name is my own?

The Railway Children

SEAMUS HEANEY

When we climbed the slopes of the cutting
We were eye-level with the white cups
Of the telegraph poles and the sizzling wires.

Like lovely freehand they curved for miles
East and miles west beyond us, sagging
Under their burden of swallows.

We were small and thought we knew nothing
Worth knowing. We thought words travelled the wires
In the shiny pouches of raindrops,

Each one seeded full with the light
Of the sky, the gleam of the lines, and ourselves
So infinitesimally scaled

We could stream through the eye of a needle.

Late

CAROL ANN DUFFY

She was eight. She was out late.
She bounced a tennis ball homewards before her
    in the last of the light.
She'd been warned. She'd been told. It grew cold.
She took a shortcut through the churchyard.
She was a small child
making her way home. She was quite brave.
She fell into an open grave.

It was deep. It was damp. It smelled strange.
Help, she cried, *Help, it's Me!* She shouted
    her own name.
Nobody came.
The churchbells tolled sadly. Shame. Shame.

She froze. She had a blue nose.
She clapped her hands.
She stamped her feet in soft, slip-away soil.
She hugged herself. Her breath was a ghost
    floating up from a grave.
Then she prayed.

But only the moon stared down
    with its callous face.
Only the spiteful stars sniggered, far out in space.
Only the gathering clouds
threw down a clap of thunder
like an ace.
And her, she was eight, going on nine.
She was late.

Lost Days

STEPHEN SPENDER

Then, when an hour was twenty hours, he lay
Drowned under grass. He watched the carrier ant,
With mandibles as trolley, push in front
Wax-yellow specks across the parched cracked clay.
A tall sun made the stems down there transparent.
Moving, he saw the speedwell's sky blue eye
Start up next to his own, a chink of sky
Stamped deep through the tarpaulin of a tent.
He pressed his mouth against the rooted ground.
Held in his arms, he felt the earth spin round.

The Climb and the Dream

VERNON SCANNELL

The boy had never seen the tree before;
He thought it was a splendid one to climb,
The branches strong enough to take far more
Than his slight weight; and, while they did not rhyme
In perfect echoes of each other's shape,
They were arranged in useful patterns which
He found as thrilling as a fire-escape.
Now was his chance! He hopped across the ditch
And wriggled underneath the rusty wire,
And then he found himself confronted by
The lofty challenge, suddenly much higher
Now he was at its foot. He saw the sky
Through foliage and branches, broken like
A pale blue china plate. He leapt and clung
To the lowest branch and swung from left to right.
Then heaved himself astride the swaying rung.
With cautious hands and feet he made a start
From branch to branch; dust tickled in his throat.
He smelt the dark green scent of leaf and bark;
Malicious thorny fingers clutched his coat
And once clawed at his forehead, drawing blood.
Sweat drenched his aching body, blurred his eyes,
But he climbed up and up until he stood
Proud on the highest bough and, with surprise,
Looked down to see the shrunken fields and streams
As if his climb had re-created them;
And he was sure that, often, future dreams
Would bring this vision back to him. But then
A sudden darkening came upon the sky,
He felt the breeze grow burlier and chill,
Joy drained away. And then he realized why:

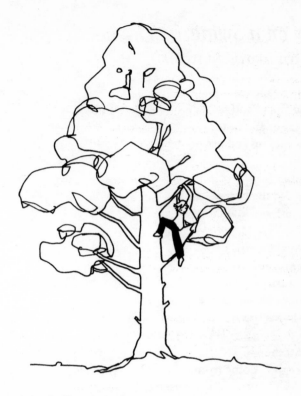

This was a tree he'd scaled, and not a hill—
The journey down would not be easier
But much more difficult than his ascent:
The foothold surfaces seemed greasier
And less accessible, and he had spent
Much of strength, was very close to tears,
And sick with fear, yet knew he must go down.
The thing he dreamt about in after-years
Was not the moment when he wore the crown
Of gold achievement in the highest bough
Above the common world of strife and pain,
But the ordeal of dark descent, and how
He sobbed with joy to reach safe earth again.

Boy on a Swing

OSWALD MBUYISENI MTSHALI

Slowly he moves
to and fro, to and fro,
then faster and faster
he swishes up and down.

His blue shirt
billows in the breeze
like a tattered kite.

The world whirls by:
east becomes west,
north turns to south;
the four cardinal points
meet in his head.

    Mother!
Where did I come from?
When will I wear long trousers?
Why was my father jailed?

The Schoolboy

WILLIAM BLAKE

I love to rise in a summer morn
When the birds sing on every tree;
The distant huntsman winds his horn,
And the skylark sings with me.
O! what sweet company.

But to go to school in a summer morn,
O! it drives all joy away;
Under a cruel eye outworn,
The little ones spend the day
In sighing and dismay.

Ah! then at times I drooping sit,
And spend many an anxious hour,
Nor in my book can I take delight,
Nor sit in learning's bower,
Worn thro' with the dreary shower.

How can the bird that is born for joy
Sit in a cage and sing?
How can a child, when fears annoy,
But droop his tender wing,
And forget his youthful spring?

O! father and mother, if buds are nipp'd
And blossoms blown away,
And if the tender plants are stripp'd
Of their joy in the springing day,
By sorrow and care's dismay,

How shall the summer arise in joy,
Or the summer fruits appear?
Or how shall we gather what griefs destroy,
Or bless the mellowing year,
When the blasts of winter appear?

Play No Ball

GERARD BENSON

What a wall!
Play No Ball,
It tells us all.
Play No Ball,
    By Order!

Lick no lolly.
Skip no rope.
Nurse no dolly.
Wish no hope.
Hop no scotch.
Ring no bell.
Telly no watch.
Joke no tell.
Fight no friend.
Up no make.
Penny no lend.
Hand no shake.
Tyre no pump.
Down no fall.
Up no jump.
Name no call.
    And . . .
Play No Ball.
No Ball. No Ball.
    BY ORDER!

My Crayon

JOHN AGARD

Do you know
with this stump
of a crayon
I can make a rainbow
grow out
of your mouth
and do a tree
like a green mop
where your neck ought to be?

Do you know
with this stump
of a crayon
I can give you
two bananas for ears
and wriggly worms
for your hair
and have blue tears
falling from the bees
of your eyes?

Do you know
with this stump
of a crayon
I can if I wish
make your nose spade-shape
your face a dish
and put two bright leaves
where your eyebrows
ought to be?

You don't believe me?
Well, just pass me
my incredible
indelible crayon.

Best Friends

ADRIAN HENRI

It's Susan I talk to not Tracey,
Before that I sat next to Jane;
I used to be best friends with Lynda
But these days I think she's a pain.

Natasha's all right in small doses,
I meet Mandy sometimes in town;
I'm jealous of Annabel's pony
And I don't like Nicola's frown.

I used to go skating with Catherine,
Before that I went there with Ruth;
And Kate's so much better at trampoline:
She's a show-off, to tell you the truth.

I think that I'm going off Susan,
She borrowed my comb yesterday;
I *think* I might sit next to Tracey,
She's my nearly best friend: she's OK.

Miss! Sue is Kissing

MICHAEL RICHARDS

Miss! Sue is kissing
the tadpoles again.
She is, Miss. I did,
I asked her. She said
something about catching
him young. Getting one
her own age. I don't know,
Miss. She keeps whispering,
'Prince, Prince.' Isn't that
a dog's name, Miss?

The Question

DENNIS LEE

If I could teach you how to fly
Or bake an elderberry pie
Or turn the sidewalk into stars
Or play new songs on an old guitar
Or if I knew the way to heaven,
The names of night, the taste of seven
And owned them all, to keep or lend—
Would you come and be my friend?

You cannot teach me how to fly.
I love the berries but not the pie.
The sidewalks are for walking on,
And an old guitar has just one song.
The names of night cannot be known,
The way to heaven cannot be shown.
You cannot keep, you cannot lend—
But still I want you for my friend.

The Lie

ALISON PRYDE

Before I told the lie the sun was shining
And my best friend had given me a sweet.
The windows of the classroom were wide open
And someone whistled outside in the street.

Before I told the lie we read a poem,
The words were rich and round, the colours bright,
Pearls and rubies trickled through the verses,
There were sparkling stars and silver moon and night.

Before I told the lie we all got new books,
Dark blue exercise, with labels for our names,
And in them we would write our favourite poems
And, after poetry, we'd all go out for games.

Before I told the lie I had a packed lunch
With tomato sandwiches and chocolate cake
And a lovely juicy peach to finish up with
And I'd share it with my best friend, by the lake.

And then I told the lie. I wasn't talking.
'No, Miss MacCavity, it wasn't me.'
And she said, 'No telling tales. Own up, the culprit,
Or I'll give you all detentions. Now, 3B,

Close your books and sit with your arms folded,
I'll give the sinner just one final chance.'
But I couldn't say a word although I longed to,
And I got more than one accusing glance.

The sun went in. And she took back the new books.
'I'll see you after school', the teacher said.
She left the room. Then someone took my satchel
And whirled it round and round and round her head,

Then hurled it through the still wide-open window,
There was a crash, a cry, 'Are you all right, sir?'
Miss MacCavity rushed in and said, 'Who did that?'
And with one voice, the class said, 'It was HER'.

The Boy Who Dropped Litter

LINDSAY MacRAE

'ANTHONY WRIGGLY
SHAME ON YOU!'
screeched the teacher
as she spotted him
scrunching up his crisp packet
and dropping it carefully
on to the pavement outside school.

'If everyone went around
dropping crisp packets like you do
where would we be?'

(Anthony didn't know, so she told him.)

'We'd be wading waist-high in crisp packets,
that's where!'

Anthony was silent.
He hung his head.

It looked to the teacher
as if he was very sorry.

When in fact he was trying to calculate
just how many packets it would take
to bring Basildon to a complete standstill.

Introspection

CHRIS WALLACE-CRABBE

Have you ever seen a mind
thinking?
It is like an old cow
trying to get through the pub door
carrying a guitar in its mouth;
old habits keep breaking in
on the job in hand;
it keeps wanting
to do something else:
like having a bit of a graze
for example,
or galumphing round the paddock
or being a café musician
with a beret and a moustache.
But if she just keeps trying
the old cow, avec guitar,
will be through that door
as easy as pie
but she won't know how it was done.
It's harder with a piano.

Have you ever heard the havoc
of remembering?
It is like asking
the local plumber
in to explore a disused well;
down he goes on a twisting rope,
his cloddy boots
bumping against
that slimed brickwork,
and when he arrives at bottom
in the smell of darkness,
with a splash of jet black water
he grasps a huge fish,
slices it open
with his clasp-knife
and finds a gold coin inside
which slips
out of his fingers
back into the unformed unseeing,
never to be found again.

Boots

MICK GOWAR

It's chilly on the touchline, but
with all my kit on
underneath my clothes
I'm not too cold. Besides,
I've got a job to do:
   I'm Third Reserve,
   I run the line.

I've been the Third Reserve all season,
every Saturday.
I've never missed a match.
At Home, Away:
it's all the same to me:
   Cos I'm the Third Reserve,
The bloke who runs the line.

That's my reward
for turning up
to every practice session, every
circuit training. Everything.
No one else does that—
   To be the Third Reserve,
   To run the line.

No chance of substitutions.
Broken ankles on the pitch
mean someone else's chance, not mine.
One down—
                    and still two more to go:
  When you're the Third Reserve
  You run the line.

When I was first made Third Reserve
my dad and me went out
and bought new boots. I keep them in the box.
I grease them every week
And put them back.
  When you're the Third Reserve—
  you know the score—
  You run the line in worn-out daps.

Absent Player

JAMES BERRY

Ball games her agony,
at rounders she was posted out
and placed at the furthest
possible position
under a tree almost.

Lost, as usual, dreaming,
she heard some vague panic noises
breaking through, as if, desperate,
the whole team were shouting
'Catch the ball! Catch the ball! Catch it!'

She slowly turned her face upwards.
She did not see the ball,
but, it aimed at a resistance
and came down straight, smack
onto a well-shaped mouth.

Her front teeth were loosened
in blood. She lay on the grass.
No way could she tell any
sympathy from boiling rage
around her. She cried, quietly.

I Think my Teacher is a Cowboy

JOHN COLDWELL

It's not just
that she rides to school on a horse
and carries a Colt 45 in her handbag.

It's not just
the way she walks;
hands hanging over her hips.

It's not just
the way she dresses;
stetson hat and spurs on her boots.

It's not just the way she talks;
calling the playground the corral,
    the Head's room the Sheriff's office,
    the school canteen the chuck wagon,
    the school bus the stagecoach,
    the bike sheds the livery stable.

What gives her away
is when the hometime pips go.
She slaps her thigh
and cries
'Yee ha!'

Children Imagining a Hospital

for Kingswood County Primary School

U. A. FANTHORPE

I would like kindness, assurance,
A wide selection of books;
Lots of visitors, and a friend
To come and see me:
A bed by the window so I could look at
All the trees and fields, where I could go for a walk.
I'd like a hospital with popcorn to eat.
A place where I have my own way.

I would like HTV all to myself
And people bringing tea round on trollies;
Plenty of presents and plenty of cards
(I would like presents of food).
Things on the walls, like pictures, and things
That hang from the ceiling;
Long corridors to whizz down in wheelchairs.
Not to be left alone.

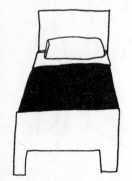

The Phantom Lollipop Lady

ADRIAN HENRI

The phantom lollipop lady
haunts the crossroads
where the old school used to be;
they closed it down in 1973.

The old lollipop lady
loved her job, and stood there
for seven years altogether,
no matter how bad the weather.

When they pulled the old school down
she still stood there every day:
a pocketful of sweets for the little ones,
smiles and a joke for the big ones.

One day the lollipop lady
was taken away to hospital.
Without her standing there
the corner looked, somehow, bare.

After a month and two operations
the lollipop lady died;
the children felt something missing:
she had made her final crossing.

Now if you go down alone at dusk
just before the streetlights go on,
look closely at the corner over there:
in the shadows by the lamp-post you'll see her.

Helping phantom children across the street,
holding up the traffic with a ghostly hand;
at the twilight crossing where four roads meet
the phantom lollipop lady stands.

The Future

SPIKE MILLIGAN

The young boy stood looking up the road
to the future. In the distance both sides
appeared to converge together. 'That
is due to perspective, when you reach
there the road is as wide as it is here,'
said an old wise man. The young
boy set off on the road, but,
as he went on, both sides of the
road converged until he could
go no further. He returned to ask
the old man what to do, but
the old man was dead.

Why Cry?

JULIE O'CALLAGHAN

You know something wonderful
will always happen.
It always does.
Know what I mean?
Like how
you just opened the window
and the warm breeze
wrapped itself
around your neck.
It will happen again.
It always does.

How I See It

KIT WRIGHT

Some say the world's
A hopeless case:
A speck of dust
In all that space.
It's certainly
A scruffy place.
Just one hope
For the human race
That I can see;
Me. I'm
ACE!

Celebration

ANN ZIETY

is daring
to be
who we are
it's like dancing
on table tops
while the world spins
and the fear stops
and the waves crash
and the stars glow
and the heart beats
and inside your head
you hear this song
rising
up
like laughter
rising
up
like a firework
soaring and weightless
to fill the whole sky
with joy

Index of Titles and First Lines

(First lines are in italics)

Index of Authors

Index of Artists

ALISSA IMRE GEISS:
15, 21, 24, 47, 94, 99, 110, 117, 119, 129, 145, 146

ROSALIND HUDSON:
17, 22, 55, 56, 72, 77, 83, 85, 91, 121, 132, 148

KATE MOORE:
viii, ix, 19, 40, 41, 60, 64, 65, 86, 101, 112, 113,
114, 115, 127, 138, 150, 151

LAURA STODDART:
11, 28, 37, 49, 63, 68, 88, 107, 143

SARAH YOUNG:
contents, 13, 27, 31, 34, 38, 42, 43, 45, 51, 53,
59, 70, 74, 75, 78, 79, 80, 81, 92, 97, 105,
108, 109, 123, 130, 135, 136, 141, index

Acknowledgements

JOHN AGARD: 'My Crayon' from *Grandfather's Old Bruk-a-Down Car* (Bodley Head, 1994) and 'The Older the Violin the Sweeter the Tune' from *Say It Again, Granny* (Bodley Head, 1986), reprinted by permission of John Agard c/o Caroline Sheldon Literary Agency.

MAYA ANGELOU: 'Willie' from *Collected Poems* (Virago), reprinted by permission of Little, Brown and Company, London; and from *And Still I Rise*, copyright © 1978 Maya Angelou, reprinted by permission of Random House, Inc.

W. H. AUDEN: 'Twelve Songs, I' ('Say this City has Ten Million Souls') from *Collected Poems*, copyright © 1940 and renewed 1968 by W. H. Auden, reprinted by permission of Faber & Faber Ltd and Random House, Inc.

GERARD BENSON: 'The Busker' and 'Play No Ball' from *The Magnificent Callisto* (Viking 1992), reprinted by permission of the author.

JAMES BERRY: 'Seeing Granny', 'One', and 'Mum Dad and Me' from *When I Dance* (Hamish Hamilton, 1988), copyright © James Berry 1988; 'Watching a Dancer' and 'Absent Player' from *Playing the Dazzler* (Hamish Hamilton, 1996), copyright © James Berry 1996, all reprinted by permission of PFD on behalf of James Berry.

ANN BONNER: 'My Little Sister', copyright © Ann Bonner, from Brian Moses (ed.): *You Just Can't Win* (Blackie, 1991), reprinted by permission of the author.

RICHARD BRAUTIGAN: 'The Chinese Checker Players' from *The Pill Versus the Springhill Mine Disaster*, copyright © 1965 Richard Brautigan, reprinted by permission of Houghton Mifflin Company. All rights reserved.

MARK BURGESS: 'Grandpa Never Sleeps' from *Can't Get to Sleep* (Methuen Children's Books, an imprint of Egmont Children's Books Ltd, London, 1990), copyright © Mark Burgess 1990, reprinted by permission of the publishers.

CHARLES CAUSLEY: 'Cowboy Song' and 'Who?' from *Collected Poems 1951-2000* (Macmillan), reprinted by permission of David Higham Associates.

LEONARD CLARK: 'Montana Born' from *The Broad Atlantic* (Dobson Books Ltd), reprinted by permission of Robert Clark, Literary Executor.

GILLIAN CLARKE: 'Anorexic' from *P N Review* (Carcanet Press Ltd), reprinted by permission of the publishers.

JOHN COLDWELL: 'I Think my Teacher is a Cowboy' first published in *Read Me* (Macmillan), reprinted by permission of the author.

JOHN CORBEN: 'Sunday Fathers' first published in Michael Harrison: *Junk Mail* (OUP, 1995), reprinted by permission of Michael Harrison.

JOHN COTTON: 'Torches' from *The Crystal Zoo* (OUP, 1965), reprinted by permission of the author.

JUNE CREBBIN: 'The Whistler' from *Dinosaur's Dinner* (Viking, 1992) and 'My Grannies' from *The Jungle Sale* (Viking, 1988), both copyright © June Crebbin, reprinted by permission of the author.

CAROL ANN DUFFY: 'Stealing' from *Selling Manhattan* (1987), reprinted by permission of the publisher, Anvil Press Poetry Ltd; 'Lies' and 'Late' from *Meeting Midnight* (2000) reprinted by permission of the publisher, Faber & Faber Ltd.

U. A. FANTHORPE: 'Children Imagining a Hospital' from *Neck-Verse* (Peterloo Poets, 1992), copyright © U. A. Fanthorpe 1992, reprinted by permission of the publisher.

JOHN FENNIMAN: 'The Salesman' and 'Bedtime' both first published in this collection by permission of Michael Harrison.

ROSANNE FLYNN: 'The City People Meet Themselves' from Jennifer Curry (ed.): *Wondercrump Poetry!* (Red Fox, 1995), reprinted by permission of The Random House Group Ltd.

ROY FULLER: 'Child Wondering' from *Seen Grandpa Lately?* (Deutsch, 1972) and 'The Dark' from *Poor Roy* (Deutsch, 1977), both reprinted by permission of John Fuller.

MICK GOWAR: 'Boots' from *Third Time Lucky* (Viking Kestrel, 1988), copyright © Mick Gowar 1988, reprinted by permission of Penguin Books Ltd and the author.

PHILIP GROSS: 'People-in-Cars', 'Dirge for Unwin' and 'Multi Storey' from *The All-Nite Café* (1993), reprinted by permission of the publishers, Faber & Faber Ltd.

SEAMUS HEANEY: 'The Railway Children' from *Station Island* (1984), copyright © Seamus Heaney 1984, reprinted by permission of the publishers, Faber & Faber Ltd and Farrar, Straus & Giroux, LLC.

JOHN HEGLEY: 'Eddie Don't Like Furniture' from *Can I Come Down Now, Dad?* (Methuen, 1991), copyright © John Hegley 1991; 'Uncle and Auntie' and 'The Death of a Scoutmaster' from *Glad to Wear Glasses* (Deutsch, 1990), copyright John Hegley 1990, all reprinted by permission of PFD on behalf of John Hegley.

PHOEBE HESKETH: 'Sally' from *A Song of Sunlight* (Bodley Head), reprinted by permission of The Random House Group Ltd.

ADRIAN HENRI: 'The Phantom Lollipop Lady', 'The Lurkers', and 'Best Friends' from *The Phantom Lollipop Lady* (Methuen, 1989), copyright © 1989 Adrian Henri, reprinted by permission of the author c/o Rogers, Coleridge & White Ltd, 20 Powis Mews, London W11 1JN; 'Ideal Gnome' from *Rhinestone Rhino* (Methuen, 1989), reprinted by permission of Catherine Narcangeli.

RUSSELL HOBAN: 'My Friend Thelma' from Anne Harvey (ed.): *Six of the Best: A Puffin Sextet of Poets* (1989) reprinted by permission of David Higham Associates.

MARY ANN HOBERMAN: 'Brother' from *The Llama Who Had no Pajama: 100 Favorite Poems* (Harcourt Brace), copyright © 1959, renewed 1987, 1998 by Mary Ann Hoberman, reprinted by permission of Gina Maccoby Literary Agency and Harcourt, Inc.

A. E. HOUSMAN: 'Purple William' from *The Complete Poems of A. E. Housman* (Jonathan Cape, 1959), reprinted by permission of The Society of Authors as the literary representative of the Estate of A. E. Housman.

LANGSTON HUGHES: 'Aunt Sue's Stories' from *Selected Poems*, copyright © by the Estate of Langston Hughes, reprinted by permission of David Higham Associates Ltd and Alfred A. Knopf, a division of Random House, Inc.

TED HUGHES: 'Work and Play' from *Season Songs* (1976), reprinted by permission of the publishers, Faber & Faber Ltd.

ROBERT HULL: 'For the Child Who Became Christopher' from *Encouraging Shakespeare* (Peterloo Poets, 1993), copyright © Robert Hull 1993, reprinted by permission of the publisher.

JACKIE KAY: 'New Baby' and 'I'm Not Old Enough Yet' from *Two's Company* (Blackie, 1992), copyright © Jackie Kay 1992, reprinted by permission of Penguin Books Ltd; ...don Gallacher' first published in *Read Me* (Macmillan) reprinted by permission of ...he author.

...he Man Who Wasn't There' and 'Cold Feet' from *Late Home* (Viking ... permission of the author.